Stick something here

Hendrix regularly smashed up and set fire to his guitar.

JON BON JOVI HAS STARRED IN 18 FILMS INCLUDING, YOUNG GUNS II, MOONLIGHT AND VALENTINO THE LEADING MAN, VAMPIRES: LOS MUERTOS.

Stick something
here

Stick something
here

Springsteen's shows have been known to last up to four hours!

Quipped Crowther: 'When Phil asked for Caroline's hand in marriage, I said, "Why not – you've had all the rest of her".'

Leslie Crowther on
Phil Lynott (Thin Lizzy)

In the course of history the **Rolling Stones** and countless other major groups are essentially loved, but **the Beatles** are universally and unconditionally adored.

Mick Jagger has starred in 11 films including, Performance, Ned Kelly, Enigma, Mayor of the Sunset Strip.

Stick something
here

Stick something
here

Michael Hutchence became a tabloid goldmine in the 1990s when he had an affair with Paula Yates, who was at the time married to the saintly Bob Geldof. They had a daughter called Heavenly Hiraani Tiger Lily.

Queen's Greatest Hits album spent an amazing 450 weeks in the album charts after entering at number one.

Stick something
here

Stick something
here

'Basically rock stardom comes down to the cut of your trousers.'

David Bowie

THE DARKNESS DEBUT ALBUM, 'PERMISSION TO LAND' WENT QUADRUPLE PLATINUM WITH RECORD SALES MORE THAN 1.2 MILLION.

Stick something
here

Stick something
here

Bon Jovi's 'Slippery When Wet' album was inspired by the band's experience at a local strip club!

Richie Sambora got his first guitar when he was 12 and is best known for his work with Bon Jovi.

Jimmy Page was one of London's most in-demand session guitarists before he formed Led Zeppelin, the most influential band of the seventies.

Stick something
here

Santana has sold more than 50 million albums.

"Being in **Fleetwood Mac** is more like being in **group therapy.**"

Mick Fleetwood

Eddie Van Halen is the guitarist on
Michael Jackson's 'Beat It.'

Stick something
here

Stick something
here

David Bowie
has released 37
original albums

'MY TEETH — I DON'T LIKE HOW THEY STAND OUT. I ALWAYS THINK OF ARRANGING THEM BUT I DON'T HAVE TIME. BESIDES, I'M PERFECT.'

Freddie Mercury

Stick something
here

Meat loaf has starred in 30 films: Fight Club, The Rocky Horror Picture Show and Wayne's World.

Fans have turned the site of Marc Bolan's fatal car crash on Putney common into a shrine, and on the anniversary of his death each year it is festooned with flowers, candles and pictures.

The Guns 'N' Roses frontman Axl Rose once famously challenged Nirvana's Kurt Cobain to a fight at the 1992 MTV music awards.

"Slash from Guns 'N' Roses played
guitar on two tracks from 'Mama Said'
by Lenny Kravitz."

'Layla' was written about Eric Clapton's love for George Harrison's then-wife Pattie Boyd Harrison.

Stick something
here

'My interest in music dissipated during the eighties as I realised that I was more important.'
David Bowie

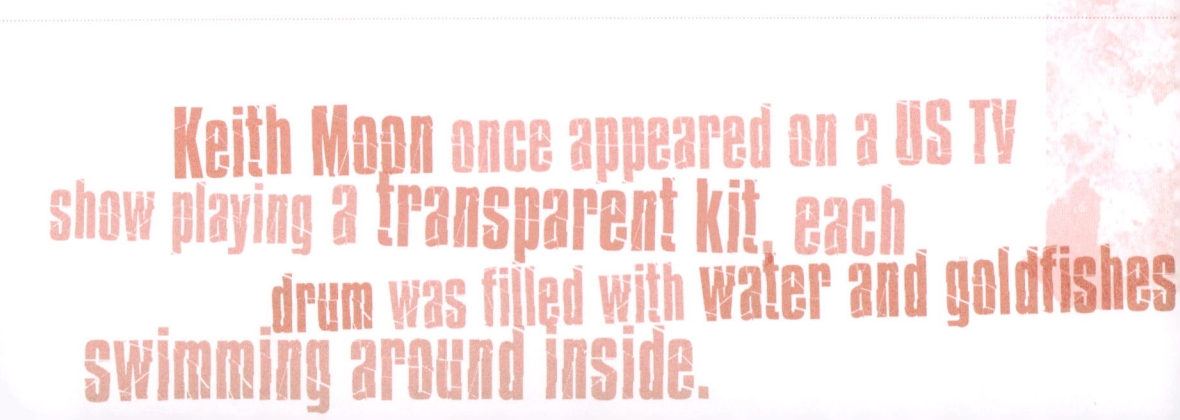
Keith Moon once appeared on a US TV show playing a transparent kit, each drum was filled with water and goldfishes swimming around inside.

Stick something
here

"I've never had problems with drugs. I've had problems with the police."

Keith Richards
(The Rolling Stones)

'I'VE GOT PEOPLE WHO WANT TO KILL ME AND PEOPLE WHO WANT TO MAKE LOVE TO ME, JUST SO THEY CAN SELL THEIR STORIES TO THE NEWSPAPERS.'

Bono

Stick something
here

'Bohemian Rhapsody' was Freddie's most creative statement and he got fed up with people asking him to explain its meaning.

Mick Jagger is an actor, writer, songwriter, producer, businessman and cricket fan, and was knighted in 2003 for his services to popular music.

Linkin Park's album 'Meteora' entered the Billboard charts at number one after selling 810,000 copies in its first week.

Selling over 140 million albums and counting, AC/DC remains one of the purest and most successful bands in rock 'n' roll.

Stick something here

Stick something
here

Ace Frehley has released 47 albums with Kiss, and seven solo albums – an impressive 54 in total.

When Jim Morrison died in Paris in 1971 he was
facing indecency charges for having exposed
himself on stage at a concert in Florida.

Stick something
here

Jimi Hendrix died
In a flat in London's
Notting Hill in 1970.

'MARILYN MANSON? YEAH, REALLY
ORIGINAL. STICK SOME
MAKE-UP ON AND GIVE YOURSELF A
GIRL'S NAME. THAT'S NEVER
BEEN DONE.'

Alice Cooper

Stick something
here

'There are only **two bands** in the whole world that are any good - us and **Motörhead.**'

Dee Dee Ramone, The Ramones

Faster than the speed of light on his souped-up
red and white striped Stratocaster,
Eddie Van Halen set a trend for long
permed hair. Fortunately it didn't last...

'Without music to decorate it, time is just a bunch of production deadlines or dates by which bills must be paid.'

Frank Zappa

Stick something
here

Noel Gallagher was born into a family of Irish Catholics in Burnage.

'Information is not knowledge.
Knowledge is not wisdom.
Widsom is not truth. Truth is not beauty.
Beauty is not love
Love is not music. Music is the best.'

Frank Zappa

U2's eleventh album 'How to Dismantle an Atomic Bomb' has sold more than 8.5 million copies worldwide since its release in November 2004.

Stick something
here

Stick something
here

Debbie Harry is the oldest female to reach number one in the UK charts with 'Maria.'

'I HEARD THAT YOUR BRAIN STOPS GROWING WHEN YOU START DOING DRUGS. LETS SEE. I GUESS THAT MAKES ME 19.'

Steven Tyler (Aerosmith)

Stick something
here

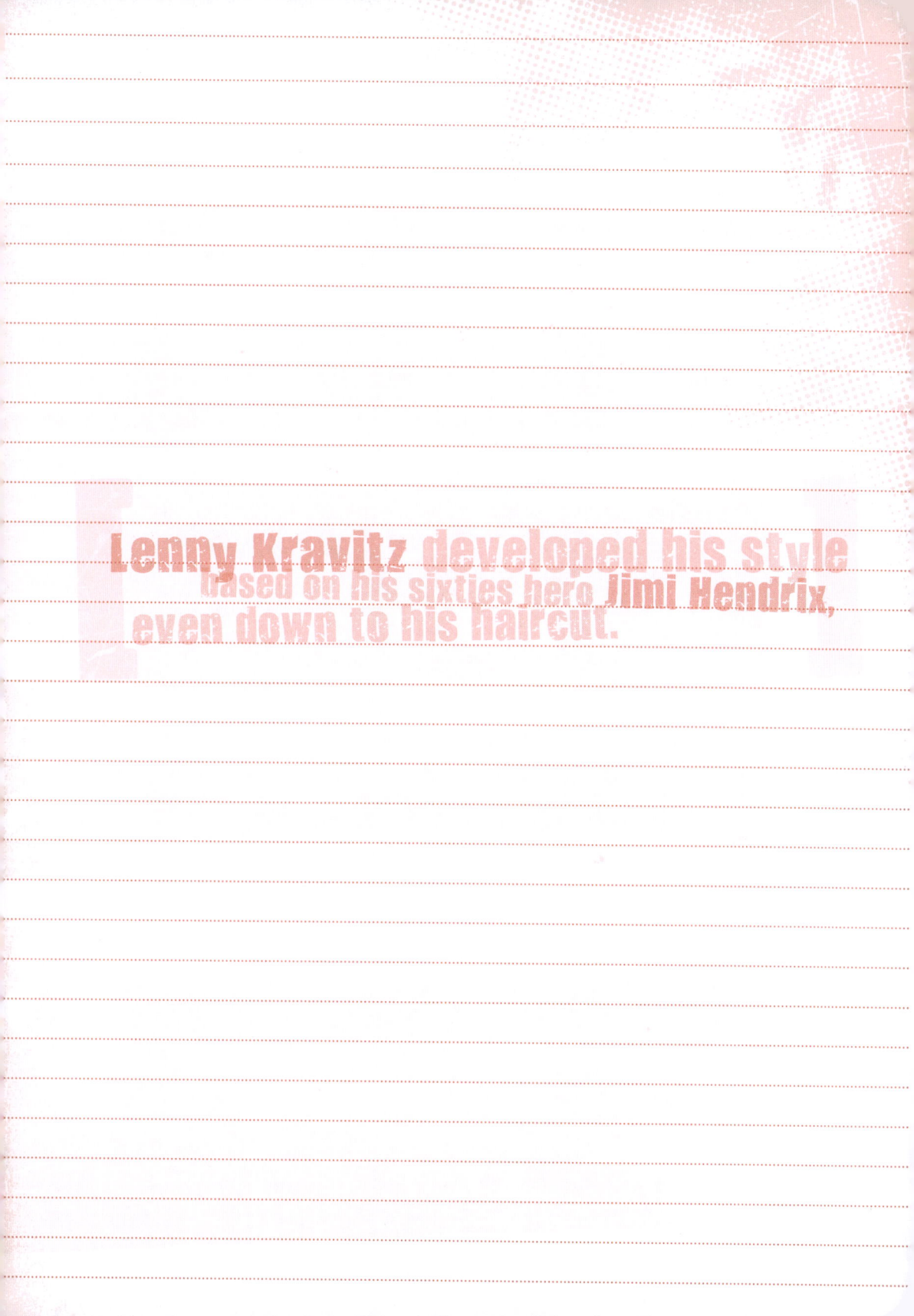

Lenny Kravitz developed his style based on his sixties hero Jimi Hendrix, even down to his haircut.

Freddie Mercury was born **Farrokh Bulsara.**
In **2004** he was ranked **number 18** in a
Forbes magazine list of the
highest-earning dead celebrities.

Angus Young is the only metal guitarist whose knees are on permanent display thanks to the school uniform he wears during AC/DC concerts.

'I won't speak to the **teen mags** because all they want to **talk** about is **hairspray** and stuff.'

Jon Bon Jovi

'I was sitting on the crapper looking at the toilet paper; and I was thinking, How come there's no Kiss toilet paper out there?'

Gene Simmons (Kiss)

Stick something
here

Stick something
here

Frank Zappa released more than 50 albums, with many more having been released posthumously.

'Mothers still hide their kids from me at airports.'

Alice Cooper

Stick something
here

Stick something
here

'prog' rock fused
jazz and classical
music with rock.

PETER DENNIS BLANDFORD TOWNSHEND WAS BORN IN 1945 AND RECEIVED HIS FIRST GUITAR FROM HIS GRANDMOTHER AT THE AGE OF 12.

Stick something
here

Stick something
here

Time and time again Deep Purple is cited as the band that crafted heavy rock to a fine art.

Published by

Omnibus Press

14-15 Berners Street, London W1T 3LJ, UK.

Exclusive Distributors:

Music Sales Limited

Distribution Centre, Newmarket Road, Bury St Edmunds, Suffolk IP33 3YB, UK.

Music Sales Corporation

257 Park Avenue South, New York, NY 10010, USA.

Music Sales Pty Limited

20 Resolution Drive, Caringbah, NSW 2229, Australia.

Australian Booktrade:

Macmillan Distribution Services, 56 Parkwest Drive, Derrimut, Vic 3030, Australia.

Order No. OP53240
ISBN 978-1-84938-161-1

www.musicsales.com

This book was conceived, designed, and produced by
Paperwasp, an imprint of Balley Design Limited,
The Mews, 16 Wilbury Grove, Hove, East Sussex, BN3 3JQ, UK.
www.paperwaspbooks.com

Creative director: Simon Balley
Designer: Andrew Li

Printed in China